# Flowin

## Shontel D. Hightower

authorHOUSE®

*AuthorHouse™*
*1663 Liberty Drive*
*Bloomington, IN 47403*
*www.authorhouse.com*
*Phone: 1-800-839-8640*

*Published by AuthorHouse  9/26/2012*

*ISBN: 978-1-4772-5571-1 (sc)*
*ISBN: 978-1-4772-5572-8 (e)*

*Library of Congress Control Number: 2012914118*

# Table of Contents

# DRAMA!

I had so much drama during the course of one life time

That I promised myself no-more Drama

Like my girl Mary J. said

There comes a time when the DRAMA is not entertaining anymore

There comes a time that if my best is not good enough.

Then there is the door.

I promised myself. **NO-More!**

**No More Drama!**

I try to live a peaceful life.

But here go Drama trying to come back in

God came to give me peace

and here you go Drama

Trying to release your issues on me

Drama!

No not today

I'm seriously running from you this time

This is not 1999 when I lived for the drama and loved the drama

This is a new day and a new season

Drama I don't even want to meet you

You are so full of it

Thinking this is what I want

You aren't anything but a big front

Acting like you down for me

But in the back of your mind you were sent to KILL me with the Drama

So here I am telling you the truth

Drama!

I don't want or need you

I don't want you!

I don't want you!

You stress me

I'm not pressed to have you in my life

Drama

Get Back

Go away

You're not attractive to me

Get behind me and flee!

I'm done!

**I'm Free from the Drama!**

# Falling

Sometimes I feel like I'm falling
Falling out of the will of God
Falling away from the Glory!

## Falling

Am I falling out of love with you?
You had my back time and time again
You show yourself faithful to me
You give me dreams of things to come
How could this be?
I want to see you in eternity

Falling out of love with you is not something I want to do
Falling to the thoughts in my mind that you did not give me
Falling away is what it seems
Then I had to realize I'm here with you
You have my heart and my soul
### You are the one who gave me goals

## Falling

Only you have the Power to keep me from falling
Only you

In your presence I'm falling
In your Glory I'm falling
In your will I'm falling
I'm here falling

There's no other way to fall

You present me faultless
You see me for who I really am
And I thank you
Keep me falling for you

# Falling

# Hello

Here you go again

You making my head spin

You given me all this drama

You must think I'm you Baby Mama

I was digging you and all of that but your convo

Is all wack

Hold on that's my other line

*Hello*

I think you going to be my new boo

The other line is holding but I think I am going to let that go and make my dreams come true

I no longer want to be his

Hold on

Hello, baby I'm back it's time that I keep it real

I have someone else and he's got my attention

You're yelling at me

Baby you got to go

I don't have time for the drama you bringing me

All that crap you're giving me

See, the one on the other line

He's not bringing me all of this

Life is short and you acting like a misfit

Baby, I got to go

Hello thanks for holding

Are you on your way over?

Can't wait to see you at my door

Hello!

Hello!

Hello!

Baby I just had to let you go bringing me all that drama

Oh no, I'm not your baby Mama

Hello!

Baby, I sure got to let you go

Let you go! Let you go!

Hello is now goodbye

Got to let you go I'm no longer on this ride

Goodbye!

# Disqualify

You tried to disqualify me

By back biting

I thought we were running this race together

I thought we were on the same team

You telling me I'm not all that

Set her aside

And let another rise

*Disqualify Her*

She only has potential

Yes she's anointed and I see God's glory all on her

But sit her down

She can't out shine me

I'm in charge

Can't you see my big ego?

It's over shadowing the room

It's enormous that's why

I have to disqualify you

No I'm not going to promote you

Again, I'm the one in charge

Foolish thinking on my part I thought the purpose was God's glory

Apologies Mr. Ego

Here I am ready set go

I'm still going ahead

You had to say disqualify me

You don't have the right

I don't have to prove myself

Let God deal with all of that

Disqualify

No never that

As long as God is God I'm going to keep running this race

Like an athlete should

But I tell you this you need to stop all of this ego

Before you be the one DISQUALIFIED!

# Star

All my life my mama said I would be a star

Hollywood is where she's going

She spoke that over my life

Star is what Shon will be

I can see her on the big screen fulfilling her dream

Dancing, acting, and all that God created her to be

Can't you see her light shining from afar?

Yes

That girl is going to be a star

God given talent is what she has

Her future is tight and she got the right stuff to go along her journey

Yes

My mama said it

That's Shonny she's my Star

# Lust

Hi, my name is Lust

I don't want you to know my real intentions

I want to wine, dine, and take you out

I want you to think there is something special about me

I'm tall and handsome, and it is you I want

After I have calmed your nerves and you think I really want to get to know you

That's when I'll make my move

Can I come over just to chill and relax?

Put on a movie and we can chat

I'm not like any other

I promise!

That's why my name is Lust

Cause I'm going to show you

Thanks for opening the door and letting me in

Now I will show you what I'm really about

Can I touch you?

Oh

Are you telling me NO?

Get over here I just want to hold you

I promise that's all I'm going to do

Didn't you know my name is Lust? I came over here to get you?

Oh!

You really going to tell me NO

Who do you think you are?

I'm the one everyone wants

You let me come over so you can taunt me

Do you know who I am?

You know what it was hitting for

I'm the one everyone adores

Its Lust baby

You better recognize

I'm so mad right now I should smack you in the face

You let me come over to your place and you tell me NO!

Are you crazy?

I'm out of here I got to go

There is always someone else who wants me

Remember my name is Lust!

# Stalker

When I first met you

I could not get you out of my mind

All night conversations

Falling asleep on the phone

Just hearing you breathe was exciting

A few months go by and my feelings start to grow

Thinking of what it would be like in a serious relationship with you

I never thought you would be a stalker

The true you is starting to unveil

All of a sudden everything is bothering you

What's going on?

This is not the type of relationship I want

It's time to let this go

Oh no

Is what you said

Over my dead body

Girl didn't I tell you

You were the one for me

I'm sorry for what I said

I didn't mean to get mad and throw a loaf of bread

Across the room at you

Man you must have bumped your head

I'm out of here

Stalker

You constantly ringing my phone

Driving pass my crib

You going to make me call the cops

Would you please stop?

Stalker

Don't come around here no more

I don't want crazy at my door

Get a grip and stop stalking

It's not attractive

*Stalker!*

# Can't you see?

I'm living a dream

Doing exactly what I'm called to be

Expressing myself and being me

Can't you see me meeting the president?

And being a blessing to millions

Cant' you see me

Creating jobs in our community

Taking a group on a trip overseas

Can't you see me?

Living the dream that God gave me

Owning my own company and just being me

Now that be me

Can't you see me?

Moving out of the Hood

But never forgetting where I'm from

Trust that would be dumb

---

Going around the world and motivating people to be who God created
them to be

Can't you see?

All the open doors God has for me

Can't you see?

# Flow

Just go with the flow

Stop trying to figure everything out

Go with the flow

Stop having so many doubts

Go with the flow

Let life surprise you

You can't be in control all the time

Just flow

Flow

# Fun

Can we just have some fun and chill?

Do we have to be so serous all the time?

Life is short

And I just want to have some fun

Take a few trips and let the breeze blow through my hair

Go to the beach and let my feet get wet

Can we have some fun and watch a comedy?

I have so much stress going on from day to day

I just want to have some fun

How about this

Let's dance to the drummers beat

Let the rhythm move me

Fun!

Is all that I wan to do

Today it's all about fun

Let's take a ride and just check out the scenery

Fun!

Is what it is about?

I'm tired of being serious day in and day out

Let's just do something different for a change

Let's change the name of the game

Let's have some fun

# Games

Game that's all you know how to do

Can't you just be real and true?

I feel like I'm at a masquerade party

Because of all the game

Who are you for real?

Do you even know?

You play so much

You lost yourself a long time ago

Running game for so long

You actually think your name is

Game

After a while the game will be you

So stop playing before you get caught up in the

Game

# Who am I?

Who am I?

You ask!

Who does she think she is?

Does she think that she is all that?

Walking around here with her head held high

Does she think she's better than us?

It's something different about her

She stands out

There is a glow about her

Who am I?

Flip it!

I stand in the mirror and look at myself

I see a woman

Women who have been through a lot

Who am I?

As I continue

I'm strength!

I'm a survivor!

I'm a warrior!

Who am I?

I am who God created me to be

I'm someone's daughter

I'm a friend

I'm a hard worker

Who am I?

I promise I don't want anything from you

I only want to be me

And being me I promise it's not taking anything from you

Who am I?

I am me!

And I'm ok with that

Who am I?

I am fearfully and wonderfully made.

And that's who I am!

# Abort

I'm pregnant what am I going to do
I have to sit my parents down and tell them.
Daddy, what are you saying?
Abort my baby!
Are you crazy?
I know you are disappointed in me
I truly do have dreams
How could you suggest I abort the life inside of me?
What if this is a writer, teacher, or the Next Top Model
Mama please talk to me

Heck no Mama I'm keeping my baby
Abortion is not an option
This is my life
Abort!
Oh no!
This child is not a mistake it has a destiny
Abort!
Are we going to get pass this?
I love you, but abortion is no longer part of the conversation
Abort, abort, and abort,
Is shall not abort what's inside of me

# Rock My World

You rock my world

Is what you said

All night I have thoughts of you in my head

Mind blowing this situation

Boy you got my heart doing all kinds of palpitations

Thinking of you all day long

This is turning into a love song

Can you feel the melody's of my heart?

Beating and beating for you

Oh!

By the way did I tell you I thank God that he laid me at your feet?

When I think of you my heart skips a beat

I have your world spinning

Like my boy Michael said

You Rock my World

R.I.P.

You keep me glowing and flowing

Rock my World

# Single

Here you go!
Asking me why I'm single
It's not a curse
You looking at me like I'm an out cast
Again asking me why none of my relationships last

Single

Do you really think I want to be alone?
It's not my fault no one special has come along

Single

No one to go to holiday parties with
No one to talk to late at night
No one to disagree with
Then make up

Single

No one to have dinner with

Single

Do you think I enjoy this?
Stop looking at me with speculations
I did not choose the single life
So stop your silly talk

Single

Yes she's single and guess what?
I'm getting it done!

# Regret

Do you regret walking out of the door?

Because love don't live here no more

You decided to leave

You told me you had another and here is where you don't want to be

Regret

Yes, my heart is heavy

I didn't see this coming

But if this is what you want then I won't hold ya

Who am I to hold you back from what you need

Please!

Regret

Why are you asking to come back?

I thought over there is where you wanted to be

The happy couple is what it appeared

You threw away years to go over there

Regret

Live in that

It's a new day

And no I don't want you back

You had your chance to make this work

You decided to trade in love for a flirt

Do you regret walking out of the door?

I understand sorry to tell you

Love don't live here no more

Regret

# Missing You

I wish I could tell you how much I miss you

If only we could have one more conversation about what's going on in my life

I probably would not shut up

I have no one to really share my personal life with

Missing you with all the highs and lows that goes on with life

I wish I could hug you one more time

I have a hole in my heart and it's for you

Missing you

I miss your smile, your wisdom, and all of your advice

Missing you over and over again

Missing you deep within

Maybe one day we will see each other again

We were such good friends

Having each other's back

You were my rock and now you're gone

No one can ever replace you- that's why I'm missing you

# Respect

Do I have to keep proving myself over and over again?

Do you really have to make me go?

Why?

Respect!

It's hard for you to accept me as your equal

You want me to jump through hoops just to show you I know what I'm doing

Time and time again this always happens

Respect!

From the start I've showed you respect just because you are a human being

but you can't do the same for me.

Once I bring this bad behavior to your attention then you act like you don't

know what I'm talking about.

Respect is due to a dog and I'm far from that

if you can't respect me for who God created me to be

then I'm sorry I'll walk away because I respect me

Respect!

# What is Love Really?

Is love when you would do something for someone just because?

Is love when you become psycho over someone that you stop loving yourself?

Is that what real love is?

Is love fair?

Is love blind?

Is love real?

Is love faithful?

Can love just be a feeling?

Can love make you happy?

Can it?

What is love really?

Is love having butterflies in your stomach when you see your love?

What is love?

Please tell me!

What is love really?

# Motive

Motive I know you have one
Wanting to use people to get what you want
Is it possible for you to just keep it real?
Say what it is what you want

Motive

It's ok to just have pure motives
But that's not even in you to do
You tried and you were uncomfortable
Why?
You are the type that acts like you got love for everyone
But I see your true motives
You are who you are
Do me a favor and just be careful with the things that you do?
Because one thing for certain and one thing for sure
Someone will have those same motives towards you

Motives

# Missing Link

Emptiness inside is what I feel

Something is missing from my life

I've tried everything and yet there is still something missing

I tried to keep myself busy by going out with friends

And still there was a missing link

The mall is calling me so I charged my credit cards to the max

As soon as I got home I had all kinds of regrets

Missing link is what it is

Why do I feel this way?

So I prayed and suddenly I felt refreshed

Now I realize what was missing

It's my personal time that I neglected to spend with God

Now I realize I can't have that missing link again

# Bitter

Why are you so bitter?

What's wrong?

Who did it?

I get it

Past relationships failed and here you are alone

But do you have to be bitter

Are you angry at the world?

What's inside comes out

Bitterness is all in you

Is it possible to let that go?

It's a new day

Can't you see that?

Bitter

You have so much to be thankful for

You are blessed and adored

Bitter

That's not the way to go

I know you have been wounded by those you thought loved you

I get it trust me

I know the past hurts run deep in your soul

Bitterness is not the way to go

For the love of God stop being bitter

# Critical

Can you do me a favor and stop being so critical?

You are so funny

If someone else was critical of you

You would break down and cry

Why?

Oh why

Are you so critical?

You never approve of what others are doing

Sitting around judging others

Nothing is ever good enough

Can you please do me a favor?

Check your self and look in the mirror

Do you think you can start with you?

Critical!

It's not attractive at all

Next time you want to be critical of others again I say check your self-first

# Difficult

I keep asking myself

Does everything in life have to be so difficult?

Do I have to continue to fight in every area of my life?

Can it be some peace somewhere?

You live and do your best

And it seems it's not good enough

Difficult

Does every relationship have to be a struggle?

Do I have to keep proving myself on the job every day?

Difficult

Why?

Is this word in the dictionary?

I'm tired of the difficulties of life

I'm over it

*Difficult*

# Fret Not

Don't fret due to evil men
They are who they are
With all of that hate within
God has the final say when it comes to you and me
Fret not!
Keep your head to the sky
I know it hurts you to see all the wickedness in the world
With folks trying to do you harm
Take one day at a time
Keep believing God
Realize he is with us until eternity
Fret not!
Don't worry about a thing
Stay who you are don't change
People are doing their thing by being who they are
Fret not!
Let God take over he has your back
Fret not!
I know the Devil has attacks
Fret not!
Just keep doing God's thing
Fret not!
It's going to be ok

# Take Me

Take me as I am

With everything that comes along with me

Can you love me for who I am?

Take me

I'm not perfect I make mistakes

Can you let me be me?

Complex at times

Unpredictable that can be me

Take me

Please don't put me in a box

Let me be me

Why must you show frustration when it comes to me?

I'm being real

No game in me

I love me for being me

No pressure

I understand

You don't want to take the time to get to know me

You only want to see the surface let's not get too deep

I understand

Take me for who I am

I'm tired of the masquerade

Take me for who I am

# I long for you

I long to be with you

It seems like days go by without you and I having a conversation

I need you

When we don't spend time together I find myself missing you

Something in me begins to feel empty

I long for you

Today is the day that we can start over

I need you

I hope you forgive me for being selfish and ignoring you

The sweet whispers in my ear

I miss your voice

How you would share your secrets with me

I am longing for you

I want to come home

Will you have me?

Here I am

Please open up to me

I need you

I miss you

I long for you

Open the door

I'm home

I never want to neglect our relationship again

You are the one for me

Did I tell you?

I long for you

Here I am Lord

Thank you for letting me in

I've missed you

# Why

Why do you love me Lord?

Why are you kept?

Why do you stand out?

Why don't you put up with my foolishness?

Why?

Why do you have high standards?

Why are you quite?

Why do you keep to yourself?

Why?

Why do you have goals?

Why?

Why?

Why?

Don't ask me why I do what I do

Just because you don't care about yourself don't get mad at me

Why?

I could ask the same question

Why don't you change and desire to be a better person?

Why?

# Distractions

When you came in my life you seemed different

With so many good ideas I was down to be a help just to see you succeed

Distractions!

After a while I realized that helping you so much I neglected to work on my own plan

Distraction!

You became so ungrateful you overwhelmed me

I didn't see it coming

I just wanted to help another

Now I have no strength to do what I've been called to do

Distraction almost had me forfeit my own destiny until I woke up and realized that distraction just wanted to use me.

*Distractions*

# It's always something

Can we just live and be happy

Does everyone have to bring drama and negativity?

It's always something

Can we just hang out without you bringing the drama?

What's wrong now?

You look angry all the time

You never smile

Really!

You think I'm lying to you because I'm keeping it real

Wow!

It's always something you think everyone is the same with a whole lot of game

I'm too mature and I love myself too much to waste your time

It's always something

You think you got a good thing until that pretty package starts to unwrap

I did not know you were crazy

You seemed normal

It's always something

I can never catch a break

Dang

I refuse to believe that everyone in this world is crazy

Is everyone walking around in a fog?

Heavily medicated so they don't have to deal with reality

It's always something

Can we all go back to be normal?

It's always something?

# Grateful

I'm so grateful for all that I have
I'm grateful that the Lord is keeping me
So grateful
I wanted to take the time to express my gratitude
Grateful that's what I am

# Do you need a ride?

Can you get out of my life?

You don't contribute to anything

A free ride is what you are looking for

Oh, no I'm not taking care of you

You are grown

Ok I get it

You don't have goals

Please don't sit there and get upset with me

I want something out of life

I'm not ok with you wanting to be a free loader

Listen!

Please stop trying to tear me down

You have to get up out of here!

Do you need a ride?

No I'm not giving you a second chance

I've given you several already

Enough is enough

The game is over

I just don't need this energy around me

I've come too far to go back

I'm done talking I've said enough

You have to leave now

You're not good for me

*Do you need a ride?*

# I'm Free

I am free
I'm free to be whoever I want to be
I' free to do all that I want to do

I'm free

Yes that's me. Free
The world was created for me
The sky is the limit
Yes I believe
No matter who tries to tear me down?
Guess what?
Yes I'm going to keep on saying it until I die
I have a destiny waiting for me
You got it right
The negative words you say does not matter anymore
You can't come back to my door
I know longer believe in our love
I'm going to keep it moving

I'm free

Free from your opinion

Free from your clicks

Free from what you think I should be

Look at me

Do you see me?

Yes!

My name is free

# Soft Heart

My heart is soft
I'm too old and tired to play games
I know what I want and you are not it
I don't want another angry black man
Soft heart is what I've become
On the real I'm done
If another man comes to my door professing his love to me
Guess what
Ya'll going to see Shon scream
I'm tired of the false dreams
Man, stop the lying
I was just doing fine on my own
Then you come just wanting to distract me
Lord, do you hear my screams
I'm tired!
I'm done!

Is this season over?

I get it. My mother is gone

What is the point of all of this?

Lord protect my soft heart

I can't take this foolishness

All these men showing up at my door

I've suffered enough in one life time

Help me Jesus!

I need you to protect my heart

# If you only knew what was really on my mind

If you only knew what was on my mind you would not listen to me

The thoughts that I have and my dreams

If you only knew

I'm not all that I should be

Would you still listen to me?

And be all in my face trying to rent space

You want me to be fake

If you only knew

You would think I'm crazy

I try my best to stay on track

God knows I do

If you only knew

You really couldn't handle it

You would think I'm crazy

And that would be the end

I really don't care what you think

But if you really knew you would run away

I'm good with that

If you only knew what was really on my mind

You would think twice before you speak

I'm telling you the truth lying is what I don't do…

*Duces!*

# Tired

I am a woman who is tired

Tired of the foolishness and the game people play

Just tired is what I am

This has been a ride meeting different people

I can't count on one hand how many authentic people I've met

Tired!

We all have been through so much in this thing called life

I'm tired of people walking around like zombies

Calling the doctor for another prescription

I get it

Trust me I do

Don't get caught up in your head

The enemy lies there

Allow yourself to get rejuvenated

Are you tired of being tired?

If so look ahead

There is a brighter future

I'm tired of seeing you do this to yourself

Aren't you?

# Just me and you

You came in my life like a whirlwind

You took me off guard

I dreamed of the day to have someone special in my life

I started to believe it was my turn for happiness

To have and to hold

Looking at him until I get old

Someone to share my day with and all of my ideas

Just me and you

My heart started to feel warm inside

I haven't felt this way in years

Just me and you

Surprise!

You came into my life to put it in an uproar

Not real at all

Here I go again

I looked in the mirror and realized everyone does not have good intentions

This is a true fact

People come and go

You and me may never be

Disappointments in life will happen

I have to keep the dream alive

Just me and you

The thought of it may not come to pass

This is what I believe

And that's my reality

When it comes it will just be me and you

# Come Alive

Come alive
You've been living in silence long enough
Come alive and live
There is life out there waiting for you and me
We are not in the grave so we don't have to rest
There is plenty of time for that
Come out of your shell and live
Get out of the house
Get out of the rut that you are in
Smile
Be free
Come alive

# You hurt me

You shut me out for no reason
What did I do?
I tried to be an adult and tell you the truth
Is it that bad?
Open up and talk to me
You really hurt me
Even if we can never be
I'm ok with that
But if this door is closed at least let me know
You tell me I'm part of your family
Your actions show me otherwise
You hurt me
I would love to have a conversation with you
Did I hurt you in any kind of way?
Since you are not talking I will stay away
You really meant a lot to me
You hurt me by shutting down
For the record you will always have a space in my heart
I'm walking away so you can live
No more hurt

# Vacation

I need a vacation

I need to get way

I need the sun to beam all over my body

I want to sit on the beach

I need to see the clear blue sea

Yes the ocean is calling me

Vacation

It's time for a break

It's time to relax

Sleeping in sounds like a plan

No rush hour

Now that's what I need

A vacation

# I want it back

I've lost so much over the years
Today I will tell the world
I want it back
I want my family back
I want my finances back
I freely gave up so much due to foolish living
I want it back
No more delays
No more games
No more playing
I'm saying it loud for all to hear
I want it all back
No more suffering
No more pain
That's all in the past
God you said if I ask I can have
I want it all back
The enemy that plays in my mind
You are now evicted
I have no space in my head for you
All of my failed relationships
No more
All of the financial issues
No more

All of the negativity

No more

I want it all back

No more playing on my emotions

I am a Woman of God

Now more foolishness

I no longer want to entertain you

I want my mind back

I want my love back

I want my peace back

I want my life back

I want it all back

# Really

Why do you act like you love me?

Your actions show me different

Don't you realize we have bills to pay?

Here you go spending all your money on everything

Really

A relationship is not what you need right now

Keep doing you

It makes no sense how you have no regard for others

There are other people in the house

Wake up and see the light

I really need God to come in and help me

I really do

You took all my love now you asking for my money

With all your habits you are killing the family

I draw the line

Honey you really got to go

I love you I really do

This is the end of the road

I need you to get up and walk out the door

Right here today God is showing me the way

Really

This is the end

Baby I gave you chances time and time again.

You took my love for granted that's why I'm telling you to go.

# An answered prayer

An answered prayer is something I thought would never happen
After the many years and lots of tears
I thought God had forgotten about me
I would think to myself that God forgot about me
Getting upset at times and the enemy on my back
Walking around with my head hung low
After a while I started to lose my glow
Then one day the Holy Spirit came to me and said
Keep on believing
An answered prayer is what is coming your way
Don't get tired
Keep on praying I know what you need
I had to tell the enemy to back it up
God is listening to me
My prayers will be answered for all to see
So God will get all the Glory

# Family

I prayed for so long to have a family of my own
I prayed for someone to have my back
I would value you even when we don't agree
At the end of the day we could pray together
That's the great thing about family
Through thick and thin I would be there
The baby showers, weddings, and even the sad times
God created families for his purpose and on today
I want to thank you for being my family

# In the Middle of the day

In the middle of the day I love to hear from you

With all the drama that I get and the attacks that come

In the middle of the day just the sound of your voice makes me smile

Hold up!

Let me tell you

This is something you should want to do

Checking on me because I'm a part of you

I'm not trying to nag you

That's not what God called me to do

In the middle of the day

I need you to pick me up

I actually pray to God to lay it on your heart to call

No pressure

I just want our love to grow

So we can flow

Just wanting you to know that I would love to hear from you

In the middle of the day

# My Desire

I have a desire to be a wife and a mother

To see my babies be all they can be

My desire is to have a family

You see

To hear laughter in the house

Now I can hear a pin drop

I can hear every breath that I take

I pray for my desire all the time

Years have gone by and this desire has not come to pass

I dare not give up

God promised me to give me the desires of my heart

My desire is still mine

# Everyone will see

Everyone will see you bless me

I've been talked about and put down

Yes even in the church

I get the stares and the questions

What's wrong with you?

Why aren't you married?

I suck it up and take it on the chin

Because everyone will see

Yes it's hard to believe

I know without a shadow of a doubt everyone will see you bless me

So called friends and nay-Sayers in the church

Who pretend to be praying for me?

I see you!

No more delays I need you to bless me

Everyone will see you are a mighty and real God

And yes you do answer prayers

# Let it go for Real

I held on to you in my mind for years

I've prayed to let it go and the love I have for you won't go away

I've fasted and all of that

And yet I still love you

I can't be in love all by my self

It takes two to make it complete

So I see you from time to time and you still blow my mind

Can't figure out this hold you have on me

I need and want to let it go

I've tried to pray again

Then I see you with another

And all of my emotions start racing

It's obvious that you don't want me anymore

So in prayer once more

Asking the Lord to help me let it go

No longer wanting this hold over me

A decade has passed and you still got me day dreaming

I have to let this go for real

No more popping up on you

Wanting to have conversation

I can't hold on to a fantasy that will never happen

This time is for real

I can't believe my love is finally fading

I release you from the past

It's over and that's where it will stay

I wish I could have let this go sooner

But I did not want to

I had hope in us and believed

That if you loved someone long enough they would come back and feel the same

So baby it was good back in the day

But I no longer want to feel this way

Towards you that is

I'm for real all the way

It was a pleasure meeting you and spending time

No regrets

I let it go for real this time

# How can I compete?

How can I compete when you love the streets?

I've prayed for you over the years and all you do is bring me tears

I had hope for you at one point

But, how can I compete when you think the streets are so sweet

That's were your heart is

You not even trying to be about God's bizz

How can I compete?

When you trying to be in the streets

Realness is not what you want

If you don't want to serve the Lord I can understand

I've tried so many times to tell you the Master's plan

It's very clear that's not what you want

I refuse to flaunt what God has given me to see

I'm done trying with you

Go ahead and keep living on the losing side

I love you!

But I realize that's not enough

You are looking for the love of the streets

Ghetto super star that's who you are

On the real

How can I compete?

# Faded

I never thought my love would die for you

It has faded away

You killed me softly and I will never know why

I guess you will take it to your grave

Faded to black

It's really over

I never thought I would live to see this day

Maybe it was me who never had a clue

But you knew all along

The love I thought we had was never meant to be

It was never you and me

Yesterday is gone

No looking back

The love I had for you has faded

# Heavy

I woke up with heavy today

Don't like the feeling I want it to go away

I've prayed and heavy is still here

It's very hard to breathe

Heavy!

Please let me go

I want to be able to breathe with a steady flow

Then I realized it's what it is

Heavy is visiting me today

# Satisfaction

Mama used to say I'm never satisfied

I wonder why

Life is a hustle

Always trying to be the best

As soon as you get what you want you are not happy

Satisfaction

Is what you thought you would get but I bet you are living in regrets?

Love didn't bring you what you thought it would

Satisfaction is what you were looking for

Mama was right

All along I was never satisfied

I refuse to settle for less!

Why should I?

*Satisfaction*

# I need you

Lord it's me again
I need some prayers answered
I need you to deliver me
I know you came to give me life and joy
Keeping it real is the only way I know how to be
Crying every night tired and worn out from fighting
Every time I turn around here goes the enemy knocking me down
For sure I'm trying to be like you
But I feel like I'm failing you
That's why I need you
Today is a new day so please have your angels surround me

*I need you!*

No one else will do
Please answer my prayer and turn my situation around
I don't want to feel down
That's why I need you

# Granpop

Granpop I miss you so much

Ever since I was a little girl you had my back

You used to call all of us boogabear

I really miss your food

Boy you really could cook

Oh what a treat

I would not miss your dinners for the world

Granpop

You were the best and I'll never forget you

The way you used to smile when you would see me

I know you realized how much I appreciated you

Your grandkids miss you

We do realize that God allowed you in our life for a season

Granpop

You were the best

Looking at you we realized what a man should be

Missing you so much

You were the best granpop a girl could ask for

You will always be my granpop without the D

Love you

# Faith

I was told to have faith and keep running this race

I've been knocked down so many times

After a while I lost faith along the way

I'm loosing it

Can't see it no more

Praying to God to give it back to me

Faith! Wake up!

Faith!

Faith!

Where are you?

You can't give up

I told faith

I need faith

I'm exhausted

I'm weak

That's why I need you

Keep the faith

Without it I surely will die

I'm not running away

That's why I'm trying

Faith!

Come back to me

Faith!

Makes me dream the impossible things
Faith!
Has come back to me
Thank God for faith

# Scream

I want to scream and yell at the top of my lungs
I want the world to know that I get tired too
I'm not perfect no that's not me at all
Stop putting me in a box
I'm about to scream
Why are you worried about me?
Stop thinking of the foolish things

Scream!

Stop worrying about me
I want to see people set free
Get your eyes off of me
I'm about to scream
Do your best for Christ stop worrying about me?
Get your soul right
Let me be clear
Back up off of me
*Before I scream!*

# No Weapon

The darts come at me all day long

I sit and wonder why someone would take the time and try to sabotage me

No weapon!

They come so often I feel like I'm in a whirl wind

Why are you so mean?

Get out of my face

You looking crazy

Keep messing with me

Don't you realize I'm a child of the King?

The word says no weapon formed against me shall prosper

Keep throwing your darts and try to tarnish my name

The very weapon you throw at me will reverse and hit you instead of me

Don't get me wrong I don't wish you any harm

But best believe the seeds that you plant

Sweety they sure will grow

In your back yard that is

No weapon!

One thing for sure God is tired of your game

Go on and repent and get it right

No weapon will come my way

So go on and hate and keep talking smack know that the God I serve has my back

*No weapon!*

# Protect me

Father the enemy is trying to kill me

Protect me

I'm running for my life

In this dark world I need to see the light

Protect me

Keep my mouth from saying evil things

Don't see my way out

My body is tired and weak

This is why I need you to protect me

Only you can do this for me

My trust is not in man

No not this time

Protect me

That's all I need

Protection from you will guarantee me a relief

# Church Folks

I pray and asked God not to let me become church folks
I want to dare to be different
I want to be a Saint and not an ain't
Church folks!
You got it bad
They go to church just to be part of the click
A fashion show is what it really is
No power at all
Church folk!
Say I'm praying for you just to get all in your business
Then they run and tell everyone all about you
Church folk get mad if someone sits in their seat
You will get killed with the stares
Yes, church folk will ask for an envelope and put nothing in it
They do it just for show
Church folk get mad at the Pastor for not making them a leader
Church folk also will try to keep you in a box
Oh I forgot to mention they will walk past you without even speaking
You get the fake smiles and hugs on Sunday morning
Knowing they can't stand you
Church folk you are a trip
Church folk sit around and eat and drink plenty of coffee
If this is not you then Praise God don't get offended
If you are church folks

Wake up!

Change your ways it's time to get it right

Church folk!

I do not aspire to be you at all…

Church is not a social club

It's the house of God

A place to come and worship the Father

Lord help, us all to be your disciples

Wake up church!

God is coming back for a church without spot or blemish

It's not too late church folks there's always room for change

# Bless Me

I need the Lord to bless me
Sure enough bless me indeed
Bless me Lord and lead me with your guiding light
I want the world to see you bless me
Living without my blessings will kill me
It's you I want to bless me
When I'm blessed I can bless others
This is my prayer today
Bless Me

# To my Haters

My haters used to upset me

I never could get why folks hated on me

People thoughts of me used to really bother me

Haters!

Will always be there to criticize you and me

Haters!

Hate their own life

That's why they look at me

Wishing they did not have to go home to a boring life

That's right! I said it

Haters!

Get your life together

Your words no longer bother me

To my haters

Thank you for hating on me

Because of you I have the energy so succeed

So don't stop hating on me

The same hate you show to me will be shown to you

Hater!

*I no longer feel sorry for you*

# Supporters

To my special friends

Thank you for being who you are

Because of you I'm following my dreams

You've pushed me and told me to keep going

When I wanted to give up

You told me to shut up suck it up and don't give up

I thank God for you

Keep doing what you do for me

Supporters

You are exactly what I need

# Nothing can separate us from God's Love

Nothing can change my mind

I'm going to keep pressing until the end of time

Nothing can separate my love from you

I've had some sad days

In all of that I know you are there

Nothing can separate me from your love

People come and go but you oh God remain the same

It's that kind of love that keeps me going

My mind plays tricks on me my emotions do the same?

If I'm in a room full of people or at home alone I know your love is there

I know without a shadow of a doubt nothing in this world can separate me from God's love.

# Flowin

I'm going to keep flowin

No matter what

I will let the words just flow off of my tongue

This relationship I have with these words is something I can't explain

That's why I keep going

Flowin until I have nothing else to say

So I will write until the lights are turned off

I can't stop

Everyone always watching can't figure out why

It's cool

Because I'm flowin

Laid back seeing the hate

I see you

I still got love for you

I will keep flowin until I can't flow know more

Flowin keeps me going

It keeps me right and tight

Can't stop the flow

Don't even want to

I thank God that he gave me my flow

# Frustrated

Stop trying to run all this game on me

Just stay away

You should had left at hello

All you have is game

I see no difference in you

I give it to you

You really looked the part

Underneath the suit you all game

Frustrated

Where are all the real people in this cold world?

If you see me go the other way

I don't want to play the game with you

Don't ever bother me again

You win

Frustrated

# Out of town

You said you were out of town
Had me sending pictures of me
Acting like you miss me
You said you were out of town
An entire day goes by and no call or text from you
Finally you send me a picture of you
And to my surprise your house is in the background
*I guess you are not out of town*

# It happened

I never thought it would happen

Just you and me

Actually getting along in harmony

Not knowing how to act

Waiting for an outburst to happen

I finally see we were meant to be friends

Everyone tried to tear us apart

The chemistry we have

I know longer care what others think of you and me

It happened

The reality is I missed you in my life

That's why I'm glad it happened

# I used to love you

You used to have my heart
I don't know what happened
I thought we were meant to be
Look at how wrong I was
I used to love you
High hopes for you and me
The reality is you are not the man for me
With all the game you play
Out all day with no purpose at all
I heard you are a heart breaker
A real ladies man
I'm here to let you know I used to love you
Today is a new day and I'm in my right mind
How could I think you would love me?
With all the game you have I know you can't help it
The love I had for you was pure and you didn't want it
I used to love you

# Reality

The reality is I am a child of God
Pressing my way to the finish line
To live up right before men
It is very hard
Temptation all around me
No one seems real
My heart cries out with many desires
God knows I want to do the right thing
The reality is I'm trying to do my best
And often times that's not good enough
I am a child of God
He is the one that I have to answer to
With the rough days and the sadness that comes along
This is my reality
I got to keep it moving

# Do your best

Do your best to be all that God created you to be
Don't worry about the haters who see you trying
Let them look and be your energy to succeed
Do your best not to get caught up in their drama
As long as you know you are doing your best
That's all that matters
Do your best
Look in the mirror and smile
Tell yourself that you are doing your best
Later for the negativity and the folks that don't appreciate you
Today is a new day
Keep it right with no unnecessary fights
Let the pettiness go life is too short
No time for regrets
Let this poem penetrate your soul
Smile and keep doing it
Do your best

# Flowin Again

Here I go flowin again

I tried to put the pen down but I can't stop

Flowin

I enjoy what I do it is so true

That's why I encourage you to flow

Putting my expressions on paper

Everyone notices my glow

You have to enjoy life and go with your flow

Guess what?

I'm flowin again

People are watching to see if I will keep the flow

So let me set the record straight once and for all

Yes I'm flowin and I will continue to do so with God on my side all things are possible

I will keep it flowin with this poetry that I write I pray you enjoy

*Flowin again*

# Why do you care?

Why do you care what I do?

The way I look or the way I wear my hair

I don't get it

I really pray you get it together

Don't worry about me and how I'm doing it

I feel sorry for you

You care more about me then you do yourself

That's it!

Get a life!

Please!

For the sake of your sanity

Go somewhere because your life is full of misery

Why do you care?

I get it

You've given up your destiny

You are so caught up in mine that you forgot about you

Why do you care?

I'm done!

# You had to ask me for some money

How dare you disrespect me and ask me for money?

So you can chill

I've never been so insulted

That a grown man would stoop so low to ask a women for some dead presidents

It's not about the money at all

It's the principle behind the situation

Are there any men out there who is holding it down?

I really thought you were a real man but you tripped me up something bad

I work hard for what I have

Who are you?

Why did you have to mess it up by asking me for some cash?

I guess you had game from the start

A lot of things happen to me in my life

But his by far surpassed them all

I thought you were a real dude

Someone to kick it with

Now you come across as a fraud

How dare you ask me for some money?

Now all of a sudden

You got amnesia and don't remember asking me

Baby boy go run that game on someone without sense

This situation is so sad

But I'm glad to know where you stand

Duce's on the real

As I write this poem I'm still in disbelief

Remembering the words that you asked

Can I borrow some money?

You had the nerve to ask me for some money

# This poem is dedicated to Blanch Pierce (Miss You)

This poem that I write is just for you

You wasn't my biological grandma but you and me made it do what it do

We would talk about the Lord and all that he's doing

Chatting about the family and praying the Lord's will to be done

I would crack up on the inside when you would call everyone thing-ga-ma-gigga's

I could never figure out what that meant

If I ask you how you were doing you never complained

I know this to be true

So I will smile from time to time when I think of you saying

Shhhhh dot, dot, dot

*Grandma Pierce I will always miss you*

# Dedication

This book is dedicated to all of the people who have been hurt in the church. I realize that it's not easy coming just as you are because of the people in the building. However please remember you are not there for them. Please know that God loves you and when he saved you he saves you. Keep going and remember when you do go to church and folks come at you, hate on you, or offend you. Please keep in mind that Jesus Christ died on the cross for you. Give God your all and allow him to use your spiritual gifts that he has given you. You are saved for a purpose and God has a special plan for your life. I'm praying for you and I love you.

Be Blessed,

Shontel

# About the Author

This is Shontel D. Hightower's third book. Shontel loves the Lord with all of her heart. After enduring so many trials inside the four walls of the church Shontel was inspired to write this book of poetry. Shontel is determined to continue to take God at his word. Shontel is motivated by inspiring others to be all they can be in Christ Jesus.